Moral Stories

# The Blind Man with a Lamp

Om KIDZ

An imprint of Om Books International

Once upon a time, in a small town, there lived a blind man. Whenever the blind man went out at night, he always carried a well-lit lamp with him.

One dark night, the blind man left his home, carrying the lamp in one hand and his walking stick in the other. As he reached the road, he heard the voices of three men who were passing by, talking among themselves.

"Look!" one of them exclaimed on spotting the blind man. "The blind man is carrying a lamp!"

The other men laughed at this sight, which seemed strange and funny to them.

"But why is he carrying a lamp? What use is the lamp to a blind man, after all?" another man exclaimed.

"This man is not only blind but a fool as well!" the first man declared.

"Let's have some fun!" one of the men suggested to the others and called out to the blind man.

"Hey blind man! Why are you carrying the lamp?" he cried out. "Are you showing somebody the way?" he asked laughingly.

But the blind man did not reply.

“Why do you need a lamp in the dark if you cannot see anything?” One of the men asked and they all laughed loudly as they mocked the blind man.

The blind man waited patiently till their laughter had died down. Then, he said, “My good men! I’m not carrying this lamp for my benefit.”

Surprised, the men looked at each other in confusion.

"Then why are you carrying the lamp?" One of them asked the blind man finally.

"This lamp is not for me but for other people on the road. I'm carrying this lamp to help people like you, who possess the gift of sight," the blind man replied.

"If I didn't carry the lamp, you may not notice that I am blind. And I could get hurt. So, this lamp is for the careless people who may not notice me in the dark," he said patiently.

“And at the same time, it would show them the way!” the blind man said as he ended the explanation.

The three men, who had made fun of the blind man, now felt ashamed of their cruel words. They realised that they had behaved in a rude and foolish manner.

"Please forgive us, Sir! We did not realise what we were doing," they said to the blind man who continued his journey, carrying his walking stick in one hand and the lamp in the other.